Hedge Fund Strategies & Tools: Study Guide
3rd Edition

Lee (Adam) Swartz

& Jacob A. Swartz

ISBN: 1517485134
ISBN-13: 9781517485139

CONTENTS

CHAPTER 1
WHAT IS A HEDGE FUND?

QUESTIONS

1. Discuss the differences between mutual funds and hedge funds.

2. Discuss the differences between private equity and venture capital.

3. Why are incentive fees different for a hedge fund manager?

4. Define arbitrage.

5. What is the difference between arbitrage and quasi-arbitrage?

6. What types of investors can invest in hedge funds?

7. What types of assets or strategies would a hedge fund manager look for, for the basis of their fund?

8. What is the difference between weak form efficiency and strong form efficiency?

9. How does hedge fund size affect profit?

10. What is the optimal hedge fund size?

11. What happens to price when there is a decrease in demand?

12. What happens to quantity when there is an increase in demand?

13. What happens to price and quantity when there is a decrease in supply?

14. What happens to quantity when there is an increase in supply?

15. What is the difference between potential supply and the supply brought to the marketplace?

16. What is the discussion in the chapter about offense and defense regarding?

17. What is an asset class?

CHAPTER 1
WHAT IS A HEDGE FUND?

ANSWERS

1. Any investor may invest in a mutual fund, however, only qualified investors may invest in a hedge fund. A qualified investor must meet income and wealth requirements or be part of a financial institution. Mutual funds are relative value investments, while hedge funds are absolute return vehicles. The incentive fees for mutual funds include an asset under management (AUM) fee only. As a result, the costs are lower for a mutual fund, but the returns in the fund may be lower, also. Mutual funds trade in publicly traded markets where there is more capital (and possibly lower returns). Hedge funds take concentrated or unique positions in many cases that are difficult to replicate in other securities. Hedge funds may take more liquidity risk, credit risk, leverage risk and due diligence is more expensive.

2. Private equity typically deals with a more established company that has cash flows and has been in business for a length of time. Venture capital is a startup company that may not have any cash flows. Usually a VC fund is more diversified in terms of the number of companies. Both PE and VC funds may have a great deal of industry risk (specialty of fund may lean towards a unique industry such as technology, etc.). A PE fund is not diversified, so performance is the reason an investor would choose to invest in this area. A PE fund may be able to use more leverage since the cash flows are more stable and higher than a VC fund. Both PE and VC funds are long term illiquid investments lasting 10-12 years, typically. A PE fund may invest in only a few companies.

3. The incentives for hedge fund managers are used to align the incentives with the investor. If the hedge fund manager has a performance fee (20%), then the hedge fund manager will take more risk and use more of their best ideas for the portfolio. A mutual fund manager has incentive to accumulate assets to obtain a higher AUM management fee. The mutual fund manager will take less risk and worry about relative performance with an index, rather than accumulate or preserve capital. The mutual fund manager will attempt to manage returns around an index. If the index loses 48% and the mutual fund manager loses only 40%, then the mutual fund manager has outperformed the market and lost 40% of the client's wealth. A hedge fund manager will obtain the performance fee only if the fund increases the wealth of the client.

CH 1 QUESTIONS (CONTINUED)

4. Arbitrage occurs when an investor uses no capital, takes no risk and makes a profit. Arbitrage should not occur in an efficient market. Derivatives are priced assuming no arbitrage is possible. Arbitrage should not last very long if it does occur.

5. Arbitrage is no risk and no capital used, while, quasi-arbitrage does require some risk and some capital. Quasi-arbitrage is taken when market risk is driven towards zero (but not completely) and leverage is then added to increase returns. Quasi-arbitrage is a low risk trade when done properly. Leverage, however, can quickly change the risk level.

6. Only qualified investors can invest in hedge funds. Financial institutions and their managers and wealthy clients with $1 million in net capital (not including a personal home) are defined as qualified. It is assumed that wealthy clients and finance professionals can obtain or undertake due diligence and protect themselves in an environment that is less transparent.

7. Assets that are in inefficient markets or strategies with less competition would be a starting point for a hedge fund. Less efficient markets should have higher returns. If there are barriers to entry, then returns could be sustained for longer time periods.

8. Weak form efficiency states that past information is already included in the price of an asset (stock). Strong form efficiency states that old or past information, current public information and insider information is already included in the price of an asset (stock). There is no empirical evidence that markets are strong form efficient. Therefore, insider trading rules make the playing field more level for outside investors. If the playing field is more level, then more investors will want to invest. If the game is rigged in favor of insiders, then fewer investors will provide capital to the financial markets. Investors will choose markets that increase the opportunities for themselves.

9. A hedge fund can get too big for its market and end up competing against itself. This could ultimately lead to a decrease in profit.

10. A hedge fund should be no larger than 15% of the market it invests in.

CHAPTER 2
HEDGE FUNDS AND DERIVATIVES TOOLS

QUESTIONS

1. Graph a call option and determine the payoff if the exercise price is $100, and the stock price is $107.

2. Graph a put option that you have written if the exercise price is $60, and the stock price is either $65 or $45.

3. Graph the profit from going long in the futures market if the futures price is $80, and the stock price is $83.

4. Graph the profit from owning a stock if the stock price is $83, and you purchased the stock at $80 per share.

5. Graph a Bull spread with call options, if the exercise price for the stock call option that you have purchased is $30 per share, and the one written is $40 per share. Assume the net premiums are four dollars. What is the breakeven point?

6. Graph a bear spread with call options with exercise prices of $50 and $70. Assume the net premiums are three dollars.

7. What is the difference between a strip and a strap?

8. Which is more expensive, a straddle or a strangle around a stock price of $100?

9. What are the potential return and risk differences between writing a straddle and buying a butterfly spread?

10. If you expect the price to rise, which strategies would you use in the stock market, futures market and the options markets?

11. If you expect volatility to rise, which strategies would you use in the stock market and which strategies would be using the options markets? Would the strategies in the stock market protect you in every situation, even if there were an increase in volatility?

12. Which strategies would bring in net revenue in the setting up of the option position?

CHAPTER 2 QUESTIONS (CONTINUED)

13. How is a calendar spread different than a butterfly spread?

14. How is a condor different than a butterfly spread?

15. How is a bull spread with calls different then a bull spread with put options?

16. How is the payoff pattern of buying a call option different then the payoff of writing a put option?

17. If a trader buys a call option and writes a put option, this will replicate what type of position?

18. What is put call parity?

19. How is the put call parity equation different for American options?

20. If an investor owns stock and buys a put option, what is this position called? What other position does this replicate?

21. If an investor owns stock and writes a call option, what is this called? Graph this position. How does this position contrast with writing a call option?

22. What is the difference between setting up a position with put options versus call options?

23. When is it rational to exercise a call option early?

24. What is the impact of prohibiting short selling?

25. What is the process for short selling?

26. If a producer is long an asset, what is a natural way for that producer to hedge their risk?

27. If a company is naturally short an asset, what is a natural way for that producer to hedge their price risk of this asset?

28. How is a collar different then a bull spread?

29. When would it make sense to set up a calendar spread?

CHAPTER 2 QUESTIONS (CONTINUED)

30. When would it make sense to set up a reverse calendar spread?

31. How do you construct a straddle?

32. How do you construct a strip?

33. How do you set up a butterfly spread?

34. If the exercise price for a put option is $20 per share, the premium is two dollars and the stock price is $12, what is the payoff and the profit?

35. Graph the short position in the futures market.

36. What are some of the differences between trading in the futures markets versus the forward market? List five differences.

37. What is a clearinghouse?

38. What is a Bermuda option?

39. What is the difference between an American option and a European option?

40. What is an Asian option?

41. What is the value of a European call option on the expiration date?

42. What is the lower bound for an American option, for puts and calls?

43. What is the lower bound for a European call option?

44. Which types of derivatives markets are the largest?

45. Which exchanges are the largest derivatives markets in the world?

CHAPTER 2
HEDGE FUNDS AND DERIVATIVES TOOLS

ANSWERS

1. Payoff is $7 per share.

2. If the exercise price is $60 and the stock price is $65, then the put option is out of the money. If the stock price is $45, then the put option is $15 in the money.

3. The difference is $3.

4. The profit is $3 again.

5. The breakeven point is $34.

6. The breakeven point is $67 and this is equivalent to going short between $50 and $70. The losses are capped at either end.

7. A strap has 2 call options and one put option. A strip has 2 put options and one call option.

8. A straddle, since it uses at the money options.

9. Writing a straddle exposes the writer to unlimited losses on the downside. The strategy profits from a decrease in volatility. A butterfly spread limits the risk (as do all "spread" positions) to the net premium paid. Writing a straddle includes writing a put and a call option at the money. A butterfly spread involves buying a call, writing 2 calls and buying another call.

10. In the stock market buy the stock. In the futures or forward markets go long. In the options market buy a call option, buy a bull spread, and write a put option.

11. If the investor thought volatility would increase, then they could buy a straddle in the options market (or a strip, strap or strangle). In the stock market the investor could buy the stock to protect from volatility on the upside, however, this does not provide protection on the downside.

12. Setting up a bull spread with puts or setting up a bear spread with

CH. 2 ANSWERS (CONTINUED)

calls would provide capital initially.

13. A calendar spread uses 2 call options, each in a different month. A butterfly spread uses 4 call options.

14. A condor is larger and can cover a larger range.

15. A bull spread with calls requires the investor to put capital up to start the position. The bull spread with puts gives the investor capital from the start.

16. Buying a call option requires initial capital and then a positive payoff occurs if the stock price increases. The most the buyer can lose is the premium. Writing a put option receives capital initially and then the payoff is positive if the stock price decreases or stays the same. The writer of the put can lose much more than the premium.

17. This is called a synthetic long position.

18. A famous equation that drives many derivatives relationships,
$$P + S = C + PV(X).$$
The value of a put option plus the stock price should equal the value of a call option plus the present value of the exercise price.

19. Instead of equality in the equation, there will be inequalities. This will be different for stocks with and without a dividend.

20. Protective Put. This replicates buying a call option.

21. This is a covered call. The relative risk of this position is much lower than a naked call option. The covered call is less risky (though not much less) than holding the individual stock.

22. Put options are more likely to be exercised early, therefore, if put options are used in a strategy then the portfolio may have to be liquidated early.

23. An American put option may be exercised early. It is not rational to exercise an American call option early unless there is an arbitrage opportunity or the underlying stock pays out an unexpectedly large dividend. The investor then wants to trade the option for the dividend.

CH. 2 ANSWERS (CONTINUED)

24. If a government prohibits shortselling, then investors will not be able to hedge their assets. If an investor is not able to hedge then they may want less of the asset. A ban on shortselling does not prevent the price of the stock from decreasing. In fact, it may be the primary reason the price of a stock declines. If investors cannot hedge the asset they may not want to hold it. Professional money managers usually ONLY enter markets they can hedge. It is possible that a ban in the futures market prevents shorting, however, it may be possible to replicate a position with options or forwards and hedge some of the position (although not as effectively).

25. Borrow a stock first. Sell the stock and take the proceeds to buy something else (such as Oil). Collect a return on the other asset (Oil) and then pay back the loan. You did not borrow money, you borrowed shares of stock. If the stock price decreases, then you profit from the decrease.

26. Go Short. If the government bans shorting then the investor will not be able to hedge or not hedge as effectively in other markets.

27. Go long in the futures or forward markets. In addition, the investor could go long in the spot market.

28. A collar includes owning the asset, writing a call option out of the money and buying a put option out of the money. A bull spread includes writing a call and buying a call option (or buying and writing a put option).

29. An investor would set up a calendar spread if the expectation was that the stock would stay in a narrow trading range. This strategy is short volatility.

30. If you thought volatility would increase an investor might construct a reverse calendar spread.

31. Buy a call and a put with the same strike price and the same expiration date. This is insurance in case volatility rises.

32. Buy one call and 2 puts with the same strike price and the same expiration date. This is long volatility.

33. Buy a call at a low exercise price ($40), write 2 calls at a higher price

CH. 2 ANSWERS (CONTINUED)

($45) and buy another call at an even higher price ($50) with the spread between all of these calls identical ($5 spread between each position). This is a bet against an increase in volatility. This is usually considered a low risk strategy.

34. The payoff is $20 - $12 = $8. The profit is $8 - $2 (premium paid for put option) = $6.

35. See graph in chapter.

36. Forward markets do not have a clearinghouse. In a Futures market, investors must put up collateral for a system called marking to market. Futures markets have a standardized product. Futures markets close positions on set dates every month. Futures markets usually have more liquidity than forwards. In some cases, exchanges will determine special rules for traders that go short in the contract.

37. A clearinghouse makes sure each investor can pay if they write an option or take a futures position (either long or short). The clearinghouse mitigates credit risk in the contract.

38. A Bermuda option allows the investor to exercise the contract on a few dates per year (quarterly, etc.) rather than on any date like an American Option. A European Option does not allow an investor to exercise early. Bermuda is between the US (America) and Europe. Bermuda option is between an American and European Option in terms of exercise.

39. An American Option can be exercised early and, therefore, must be worth, at least, as much as a European Option. Some European Options do not increase in value with an increase in the maturity date.

40. An Asian option is an option that is based on the weighted average of the price, rather than the actual stock price on a certain date.

41. The value of the European call option on the exercise date is $V_c = \max(0, S-X)$, where S is the stock price and X is the exercise or strike price. This is also the payoff and the intrinsic value.

42. One lower bound is zero for both puts and calls. Another lower bound is $S-X$ for American call options and $X-S$ for American put options.

CH. 2 ANSWERS (CONTINUED)

43. A lower bound for European call options is the present value of S-X and the lower bound for a European put option is the present value of X-S.

44. Currency and interest rate derivatives markets are the largest markets.

45. The derivatives exchanges in Chicago comprise the largest derivatives markets, however, mergers and on line trading imply that electronic markets will dominate the future and this may mean trading might move offshore if costs are lower.

CHAPTER 3
SHORT SELLING

QUESTIONS (SHORT SELLING)

1. Graph an increase in the supply of an asset.

2. Graph a decrease in the demand for an asset.

3. If more competition enters an industry, what happens to equilibrium prices and profit?

4. If the central bank increases the money supply or starts a quantitative easing program, what is the impact on interest rates? Assume that inflation does not rise for a few years.

5. What is the fisher equation?

6. Why does a central bank want to decrease interest rates?

7. What is the impact of interest rates on commodity prices?

8. How does leverage available to investors affect asset prices?

9. If banks do not lend as much as prior to the financial crisis, how does this affect the money supply?

10. If transactions that are short-term trades are taxed more heavily than long-term trades, what impact will this have on trading?

11. If European officials tax financial transactions, what impact will this have on the United States, Singapore and the Cayman Islands?

12. If a market is less efficient, how does that affect potential profit? How does that affect volatility in the asset price?

13. Does liquidity have a price? What implications does this have for asset returns? How does this affect the strategies that hedge fund managers use?

14. If a low cost producer stops production and allows competitors to produce more, what impact will this have on the equilibrium price?

15. What is the impact of a cartel on commodity prices?

CH. 3 SHORT SELLING QUESTIONS (CONTINUED)

16. How does financing affect the price of a product?

17. How does financing affect the strategies that hedge funds use?

18. If information is not trusted and must be verified, will the announcement of important news fully reflect the asset price immediately?

19. Market inefficiency can come from multiple sources. List some of these sources.

20. If interest rates are extremely low what impact will this have on the creation of more derivatives?

21. What types of companies are chosen to short? What approaches do hedge fund managers use to decide on which companies to go short? List different approaches used.

22. What are the average returns for short selling?

23. What is the average volatility in the short selling strategy?

24. What types of risk are involved in short selling?

25. How does the risk of short selling compare with buying an index?

26. How does short selling work? What is the process?

27. What is the skewness of the short selling strategy?

28. What percentage days were profitable for short selling?

29. What was the largest drawdown for short selling? How long did the drawdown last?

30. On a graph of credit risk and market risk, where would short selling be located?

31. How is short selling the market different than short selling an individual stock?

32. Will corporate managers talk to a hedge fund manager that usually or

CH. 3 SHORT SELLING QUESTIONS (CONTINUED)

almost always has a short position?

33. If a company has 20% of the shares shorted, is this a large amount on a relative basis?

34. What rules affect short selling?

35. Discuss the history and regulations regarding short selling.

36. Which types of companies would a hedge fund manager prefer to go short?

CHAPTER 3
SHORT SELLING

ANSWERS (SHORT SELLING)

1. The supply curve shifts to the right or down.

2. The demand curve shifts to the left or down.

3. An increase in competition will drive prices and profits down.

4. If inflation does not increase the impact will be to lower interest rates in the economy.

5. $R = r + Inflation$

6. If interest rates decrease then the net present value of many projects increases (become more profitable) and companies will hire more workers.

7. Lower interest rates imply that the opportunity cost of holding non-interest bearing commodities is lower.

8. If more leverage is available to investors then asset prices will be higher.

9. The velocity of money is lower, so the money supply decreases.

10. Investors will prefer longer term trades and short term ideas will not be traded as frequently. This means that volume may decrease in the marketplace. As a result, some strategies such as delta hedging will be more difficult to implement in the marketplace.

11. More trade will go to the US, Singapore and the Cayman Islands. More jobs will go to these countries, too.

12. A less efficient market will allow greater levels of profit. Volatility could increase if the asset is traded less frequently or there is less liquidity in the system.

13. Liquidity is priced in financial markets. Assets with longer time periods for harvesting will have larger liquidity premiums (private equity, PIPES, venture capital and distressed lending).

CH. 3 SHORT SELLING ANSWERS (CONTINUED)

14. Costs in the industry will increase (Saudi Arabia oil production and OPEC).

15. A cartel will have some level of monopoly power. Production will decrease and prices will increase. Profits for the producers will be larger than a competitive industry.

16. If financing is needed for a purchase then the financial institutions (banks, credit cards, etc.) need to approve the purchase. If the inventory of the financial institutions is more than the risk the company desires, they may deny loans based on the financial institution risk preferences, not on the credit of the buyer. Credit can be pulled at any time. If credit is decreased then the price of the underlying asset will decrease.

17. If financing is not available at higher levels of leverage then some strategies will not be able to obtain capital and the market may have higher inefficiencies.

18. The information will not fully reflect the news event because the final "belief" that the news is correct must be verified.

19. Some examples include: Liquidity, credit, information, market makers, complex products, products that need financing, extremely volatile assets, unique risks, asymmetric information.

20. Low interest rates create the need for more derivatives and higher interest rate bearing investment products.

CHAPTER 3
SHORT SELLING

QUESTIONS (LONG SHORT HEDGE FUNDS)

1. How common are long short funds?

2. What types of strategies do long short fund use?

3. What types of analysis are used? List five types of analysis.

4. How do long short equity funds compare with global macro funds?

5. What was the average return on long short equity?

6. What was the average volatility on long short strategies?

7. What were the skewness and kurtosis values for long short equity?

8. What is the difference between gross long and net long positions?

9. How is the net beta long different than gross long?

10. What is the difference between long short and market neutral funds?

11. What was the drawdown for long short equity funds? How long did it last?

12. How much leverage do most long short funds use?

13. On a graph of credit risk and market risk where would long short equity be located?

14. If a hedge fund has long positions of 75% and short positions of 45%, the net exposure is _____ and the gross exposure is _____?

15. What types of strategies could the long short hedge fund manager use to decrease liquidity risk?

16. Which types of assets would be more likely to go long and which types would the hedge fund more likely prefer to go short?

17. How does long short equity investing compare with shortselling?

CHAPTER 3
SHORT SELLING

ANSWERS (LONG SHORT HEDGE FUNDS)

1. Very common, sometimes long short is the most popular type of hedge fund, comprising approximately 30-50% of the funds.

2. Some are almost always long, some are almost always short; however, on average, hedge funds are usually net long.

3. Top down, bottom up, statistical, fundamental, technical and others.

4. Long short can go across different types of stocks (within the same asset class) while global macro can go across asset classes.

5. 6.05%

6. 8.39%

7. -.11 and 3.43, respectively

8. Gross long adds the volume of long and short. Net long takes the value of long and subtracts the short position.

9. The beta or net beta of a position includes the weighted average of the beta or volatility of the position versus just the amount of the investment (gross long).

10. Market Neutral funds set the beta of the position equal to zero. Therefore, the net beta risk or market risk is zero.

11. -29.52% and 79 months

12. 130-200%

13. Above index investing with one level of credit risk.

14. 30%, 120%

15. Short only those stocks with large volumes and short stocks without dividends. Long only large stocks with a large float, also.

CH. 3 LONG SHORT HEDGE FUNDS ANSWERS (CONTINUED)

16. Long higher return (small stocks) securities and short large liquid securities.

17. Short selling has lower returns, on average. Long short has more opportunities. Usually short selling has two types: stock market short or firm specific short. To short the entire market is a macroeconomic trade. Long short and shorting a particular stock is a firm specific trade.

CHAPTER 3
SHORT SELLING

QUESTIONS (MARKET NEUTRAL HEDGE FUNDS)

1. What is the basic strategy for the market neutral hedge fund?

2. What is beta? What is Alpha?

3. What is beta hedging?

4. What is the average volatility of this strategy? How does this strategy compare to investing in treasury bills?

5. What is the average return of market neutral funds?

6. What is the skewness and kurtosis of market neutral funds?

7. What types of events would increase risk for a market neutral fund?

8. What level of leverage would a market neutral fund use?

9. On a graph of credit risk and market risk where would market neutral funds be located?

10. Compare market neutral funds with long short equity.

11. How do market neutral funds compare with short only funds?

12. What is pairs trading?

13. What was the percentage of profitable trading days for the market neutral hedge funds?

14. What was the largest drawdown and how long did it last for market neutral hedge funds?

15. What was the worst month for market neutral hedge funds?

16. Market Neutral Funds are one of the fastest growing types of hedge funds today.
    a. True
    b. False

CH 3 MARKET NEUTRAL HEDGE FUNDS QUESTIONS (CONT.)

17. If you invest in a Market Neutral fund you must be aware that
    a. Managing fees are lower than other funds.
    b. You can benefit from historical stock market returns.
    c. Your returns come from "Stock Picking".
    d. The SEC watches market neutral funds closer than others.

18. It is quite possible that the most important factor in a market neutral fund's success is
    a. Market timing
    b. Industry exposure
    c. Diversification
    d. Selection of stocks

19. An attractive quality that is true in every market neutral fund is
    a. Zero market correlation.
    b. Anomalies are taken advantage of.
    c. You will never be more than ten percent of the assets under management in a market neutral fund.
    d. You will short as many stocks as you will be long.

20. According to the table, market neutral funds have performed better than which of thw following:
    a. Global Macro
    b. Merger Arbitrage
    c. A and B
    d. None

21. Please describe how money came in and out of Market Neutral funds during the financial crisis and how many funds returns were after.

    Money came into Market Neutral funds during the financial crisis because these funds were not losing 50% like some mutual funds. However, when the US government banned shorting on financial stocks, market neutral funds were hurt. When the market rebounded many funds didn't do as well as mutual funds because they were short many companies. Money will flow into market neutral funds when times are bad and come out when they are not because investors have trouble riding through tough times and not making enough money in good times.

CH 3 MARKET NEUTRAL HEDGE FUNDS QUESTIONS (CONT.)

22. An example of a market neutral fund that specializes in a few industries would be
    a. Long Verizon short at&t
    b. Long Apple short Microsoft
    c. Long Goldman Sachs short Caterpillar
    d. Both A and B

23. Explain how you would market a fund specializing in an industry specific market neutral fund.

    Industry specific market neutral funds can be a great tool for a wealthy investor. When you are shorting a company's competitor you allow yourself to be an expert in a few companies and it is easier to make sophisticated decisions. You still have low market correlation with the exception of a very cyclical industry.

24. Managing money for an institution can be different than with a high net worth investor because
    a. Money flows in and out of the fund at a high turnover rate.
    b. Many startup funds find it easier working with institutions.
    c. Due Diligence is thorough.
    d. It is easier to get institutional money.

25. One major advantage of Market Neutral funds is
    a. Even in a down market you can make money.
    b. Beating the index is not always a necessary goal.
    c. Lock-up periods are longer than most other funds.
    d. Liquidity is never an issue.

26. Which of the following are examples of reasonable lock up periods?
    a. 6 months
    b. 3 years
    c. 10 years
    d. All of the above

27. Explain why using shorter lock up periods can increase AUM.

    Using shorter lock up periods gives more confidence to investors in many situations. People like liquidity especially when they don't know the manager at a personal level. We see that funds with longer lock-up periods and less liquidity often outperform funds with short lock-up periods and more liquidity.

CH 3 MARKET NEUTRAL HEDGE FUNDS QUESTIONS (CONT.)

28. When managing any type of fund you cannot account for
    a. Government regulations.
    b. Investors pulling money out.
    c. None of the above
    d. A and B

29. The S&P 500 index is used to evaluate the performance of most hedge funds.
    a. True
    b. False

30. Compare and Contrast market neutral funds to PIPES

    Both funds could go long or short.
    PIPES can invest into bonds.
    Market neutral funds short half their capital and long half.
    PIPES should require longer lock-up periods in many cases.
    PIPE deals are usually illiquid for 6 to 12 months.
    PIPES require working with the company while Market Neutral funds just buy and sell straight through an exchange.

31. Why would you want to manage money in a market neutral fund?

32. Since the conventional rates are 2% AUM and 20% performance fee, you don't see funds that turn away investors.
    a. True
    b. False

33. A market neutral strategy works best with large cap, mid cap, and small cap stocks.
    a. True
    b. False

34. Managing money in markets outside of the US is relatively similar to managing in the US.
    a. True
    b. False

CHAPTER 3
SHORT SELLING

ANSWERS (MARKET NEUTRAL HEDGE FUNDS)

1. Long and short two stocks with a net beta of zero.

2. Beta is the correlation of the stock with the index. Alpha is the leftover return. Alpha is the extra return (hopefully positive) after adjusting for risk in the portfolio.

3. Beta hedging involves taking the market risk out of the investment. Beta is driven to zero or minimized to lower the risk of the trade.

4. 3.92%, just over the average volatility for T-bills.

5. .95%

6. -.10 and .64, respectively.

7. Firm specific or industry risk could change. In addition, balance sheet items that the firms have in common could increase risks.

8. 100%

9. At zero beta and one level of credit risk.

10. Market Neutral uses similar strategies; however, the trade must be limited to only those positions with zero beta risk. Market neutral is a special case of long short funds.

11. Market Neutral will short 50% of the trades; however, the fund is set for beta zero not negative beta. See results.

12. Pairs trading involves the trading of two company's stock with a long position in one and a short in the other. This is a relative trade.

13. 57.29%

14. -14.93% and 78 months

15. August 2010

16. B

CH 3 MARKET NEUTRAL HEDGE FUNDS ANSWERS (CONT.)

17. C

18. D

19. A

20. C

21. The performance during the crisis was positive and these are liquid funds. Therefore, during a crisis when investors prefer liquidity money may flow to market neutral liquid transparent strategies.

22. D

23. Market correlation is lower and expertise in an industry is easier to exploit.

24. A

25. A

26. D, depending on the liquidity of the investment.

27. Many investors prefer liquid investments to give them more flexibility. Investors prefer liquidity, it is an option.

28. D

29. B

30. Both funds can go long or short. PIPES can invest in bonds. PIPES require longer lock up periods. PIPE deals are usually illiquid for 6 to 12 months. PIPES require working with company management. Market Neutral short half their trades and go long half their trades.

31. To show expertise picking individual securities and profit from it.

32. B

33. B
34. B

CHAPTER 4
LONG SHORT SPECIFIC HEDGE FUNDS

QUESTIONS

1. A long short specific fund might
   A. Long Apple and short Microsoft.
   B. Long Pfizer and short Goldman Sachs.
   C. Short JP Morgan and short Morgan Stanley.
   D. A and C

2. Long short specific funds don't have to be neutral with their capital.
   A. True
   B. False

3. One advantage to managing a long short hedge fund is
   A. Diversification.
   B. You can specialize.
   C. Lock-up periods can be justifiably longer when marketing to investors.
   D. All of the above

4. Which industries, if any, would be better than others to manage a long short specific hedge fund in?

5. Why has money been flowing into strategies like long short specific lately?

6. The threshold level or hurdle rate for many funds is
   A. S&P
   B. LIBOR
   C. 10%
   D. The 30 year US bond

7. Analysis from the economy to the company is known as
   A. Company macro view.
   B. Top down.
   C. Bottom up.
   D. Specialization.

CH 4 QUESTIONS (CONTINUED)

8. When shorting you must
    A. Keep extra cash.
    B. Write put options.
    C. Write straddles.
    D. None of the above.

9. What is the difference between value investing and growth investing? How does Top Down analysis differ from Bottom Up analysis? What are the empirical   differences between these two types of funds?11. What are the empirical differences between energy and tech hedge funds? Why do you think they are different?
12. What were the differences between multi-strategy funds and tech or energy funds?

CHAPTER 4
LONG SHORT SPECIFIC HEDGE FUNDS

ANSWERS

1. D

2. A

3. D

4. Depends on expertise, however, the ability to short is crucial for success. Therefore, finding an industry with many short candidates is important. Larger cap stocks are preferable.

5. The flexibility across sectors is valued by investors during times of higher volatility.

6. B

7. B

8. A

9. Value investing buys assets at a discount using PE ratios, market book ratios, and dividend yields. Growth investing buys assets growing faster than the economy.

10. Top down starts with an opinion on the macroeconomic conditions then goes to industry selection, and specific assets within that industry. Bottom up concentrates on companies with good products and strong ratio analysis.

11. Mean return energy vs. technology: 4.63% vs 7.54%, respectively. Mean volatility energy vs. technology: 12.96% vs 7.07%, respectively.

12. Multi-strategy funds have an average return (7.24%) similar to technology and an average volatility (12.27%) similar to energy funds.

CHAPTER 5
HEDGE FUNDS - WHICH STRATEGIES TO USE

QUESTIONS

1. What causes market volatility?

2. Are commodities an asset class?

3. Why is the reputation of a central banker important?

4. What is interest rate parity?

5. What factors affect the value of a currency?

6. Which currencies are defined as hard currencies?

7. Which currency is the reserve currency?

8. What is a commodity currency?

9. What is a dirty float?

10. What is delta hedging?

11. What is the underlying position when you delta hedge?

CHAPTER 5
HEDGE FUNDS - WHICH STRATEGIES TO USE

ANSWERS

1. A lack of liquidity, more uncertainty, political uncertainty and market manipulation are some of the causes of volatility.

2. Yes and no. It depends on your definition of an asset class. If an asset class must generate income then commodities are not an asset. If an asset class protects the investor in some economic states of nature then commodities are an asset class.

3. Credibility of a policy depends on the reputation. A policy must be credible to be effective.

4. Interest rates around the world should cause capital to flow toward higher interest rates. Countries that have higher returns should attract more capital for projects.

5. Interest rates, inflation, GDP (the number of transactions) growth rate, political uncertainty, commodity prices, international store of value.

6. US dollar, yen, British pound, Euro.

7. US dollar

8. Australian, Canadian, Brazilian currencies all increase when commodity prices rise, and decrease when commodity prices fall.

9. When the central bank does not allow supply and demand to set the currency value. All major economies use a dirty float to affect exchange rates and international trade.

CH 5 ANSWERS (CONTINUED)

10. Delta hedging protects the portfolio from small changes in the price of the underlying stock. A hedge ratio is used by computing it through the binomial or Black-Scholes model. Typically, the position will buy 500 shares of stock and write call options on 1000 shares of the same stock.

11. This is similar to a covered call and a naked call if the hedge ratio is .5.

CHAPTER 6
EMPIRICAL RESEARCH –
WHEN TO USE EACH STRATEGY

QUESTIONS

1. List the time anomalies.

2. List the factor anomalies.

3. Why is the explanation of an anomaly important?

4. What is the January Effect?

5. What is the monthly Effect?

6. What is momentum?

7. What is a 200 day moving average?

8. What is the value premium?

9. How does size affect stock returns?

10. What impact does a merger have on stock returns?

11. How is a merger with 2 bidders different than only one bidder?

12. How is correlation trading used in the financial markets?

13. What are average returns for IPOs?

14. What is the carry trade? How do you implement it?

15. What is weak form efficiency?

16. What is a random walk?

17. What is semi-strong form efficiency?

CHAPTER 6
EMPIRICAL RESEARCH –
WHEN TO USE EACH STRATEGY

ANSWERS

1. January, Monthly, Weekend, Monday, Holiday.

2. Value, Size, Momentum.

3. It determines how long abnormal returns may last and whether the returns are capturing different forms of risk.

4. On average, Small firms returns are higher than large firms and, on average, all firms do better in January than any other month.

5. The end of month (day's 16-day 1 of next month) outperforms the beginning of the month (days 2-16).

6. A stock that outperforms 6 months in a row has a higher probability of outperforming the next 6-9 months.

7. A technical trading rule that captures momentum after 10 months.

8. Stocks with value characteristics have higher returns and less risk than the index. Value stocks would have a market/book ratio under 2 or 1.5. Other value characteristics may include lower price/earnings stocks and higher dividend stocks.

9. Small stocks outperform large stocks by approximately 5% per year. After adjusting for beta risk the return difference is about 2% per year.

10. A merger announcement has a return of approximately 6-10% on the target firm in the US. Bidders in the US have returns of approximately zero. Returns outside the US are higher and returns are split between the bidder and target.

11. If there are two bidders, both lose. One overpays and the other suffers reputation effect on merger strategy for growth.

CH 6 ANSWERS (CONTINUED)

12. If two stocks have a high correlation (.9, for instance), then if GM releases information that sales rose higher than expected, this will transfer to the price of Ford stock, as well.

13. Long term studies indicate that IPOs generate abnormal returns in the first week or first 6 months of trading above 15%. After the first 6 months the next 2 ½ years find IPOs underperform the index.

14. Borrow from a low interest rate economy (Japan or the US) and invest the proceeds into a higher interest rate economy (Brazil or Australia).

15. Weak form efficiency states that markets incorporate old or past information into the stock price.

16. Stock prices should be random or the predictable part would be incorporated into some investors trading strategies. An efficient market should be somewhat random.

17. Semi-Strong Form efficiency is an assumption of the CAPM. A semi-strong form efficient market incorporates old or past information, as well as, current public information into the price of the stock. It does not include private information.

CHAPTER 7
MERGER ARBITRAGE HEDGE FUNDS

QUESTIONS

1. What is the basic strategy for a merger arbitrage fund?

2. What is the average return for the target in a merger?

3. What is the volatility of the merger arbitrage strategy?

4. What is a mean convergence strategy?

5. Do most hedge funds use mean convergence strategies? If not, what is their advantage and are they sustainable?

6. How does financing affect the merger arbitrage strategy?

7. What role does the number of mergers have on the merger arbitrage strategy returns?

8. What is the skewness and kurtosis of the merger arbitrage strategy?

9. Do investors prefer higher or lower skewness?

10. Do investors prefer higher or lower kurtosis?

11. What was the largest drawdown for the merger arbitrage strategy and how long did it last?

12. What was the percentage of profitable trading days for the merger arbitrage strategy?

13. If a target is overpriced or a merger is unlikely to be completed what strategy might the merger arbitrage fund use?

14. How does time affect the returns of the merger arbitrage strategy? If a merger takes one year longer to be completed than expected, how does that affect the returns to the merger arbitrage hedge fund?

15. What role does leverage play in this strategy? What is the average leverage in this sector?

CH 7 QUESTIONS (CONTINUED)

16. What risk factors are contained in the merger arbitrage strategy?

17. Does the bidding company influence the risk of the trade?

18. Does the location of the target company influence the risk of the merger arbitrage strategy?

19. What types of regulation affect the returns for the merger arbitrage strategy?

20. What impact do multiple bidders have on the process?

21. How is a cash merger different than a stock swap merger?

22. How is an international merger different than a domestic merger?

23. How are mergers in the United States different than mergers outside the United States?

24. How is a strategic bidder different than a conglomerate merger?

25. How is a hostile takeover different than a merger? What are the average returns during a hostile takeover?

26. A fund will face major problems in the long run if they
    a. Long the target by mistake.
    b. Speculate.
    c. Diversify their portfolio.
    d. Specialize in an industry.

27. In a year where merger arbitragers are active what other strategy would work best?
    a. Market neutral
    b. Long bonds
    c. Short Bonds
    d. Long Stocks

28. Explain the process that a merger arbitrage fund goes through from buying to selling.

CH 7 QUESTIONS (CONTINUED)

29. A fund specializing in merger arbitrage will buy the target company and short the buyer. They will only act after the merger has happened because over time speculation does not make this strategy sustainable. Over time, the buyer should lose value and the stock of the target appreciates, the results of the difference is where the fund profits.

30. A merger arbitrage fund should only accept money from those who are willing to lock their money up for a few years because these deals take time respectively.
    a. True
    b. False

31. Merger arbitrage funds that use leverage of 2X are better than those that use 1X.
    a. True
    b. False

32. In a situation where ABC buys company XYZ a successful merger arbitrage execution looks like
    a. Long company ABC and short company XYZ.
    b. Long the bonds of company ABC and short the equity of company XYZ.
    c. Short company ABC and long company XYZ.
    d. You cannot make an educated assumption because we don't know what industry ABC and XYZ are in.

33. Compare a merger arbitrage strategy to a convertible arbitrage strategy.

34. The market risk, on a scale of 1-5, of a merger arbitrage fund is 3.
    a. True
    b. False

35. Merger arbitrage tends to be correlated to the S&P.
    a. True
    b. False

CH 7 QUESTIONS (CONTINUED)

36. The average annual return since 1998 has been greater than
    a. Convertible Arbitrage
    b. Market Neutral
    c. Both A and B
    d. None of the above

37. There are often hedge fund scandals in merger arbitrage
    a. True
    b. False

38. Quasi-arbitrage is more practical than perfect arbitrage
    a. True
    b. False

39. On average, merger arbitrage funds had positive annual returns from
    a. 1998-2010
    b. 2001-2010
    c. 2005-2010
    d. 2000-2010

CHAPTER 7
MERGER ARBITRAGE HEDGE FUNDS

ANSWERS

1. Long the target and short the bidder.

2. 6-10%

3. 3.57%

4. A strategy that relies on the historical norms reasserting themselves.

5. Yes, otherwise they would be betting on long shots. A fund needs more capital if it bets on long shots (also called Black Swan events).

6. If more financing is available from banks, there will be more mergers and more investment opportunities.

7. More mergers allow more trades and this will allow more profit.

8. -.32 and 3.42, respectively.

9. Positive skewness is preferred or lower negative skewness.

10. Lower kurtosis is preferred.

11. -5.46% and 32 months

12. 75%

13. Long the bidder and short the target.

14. If a merger takes longer to complete, the returns to the strategy decrease. Time is money.

15. More leverage can enhance returns. The average leverage is relatively low in this sector, one or two times leverage.

16. Credit risk, legal risk, legislative risk, government policy risk, international or currency risk could be factors.

17. If the merger is financed with a stock trade instead of cash, this will increase the risk in the merger substantially.

CH 7 ANSWERS (CONTINUED)

18. The country or state of incorporation affects the probability. The states of Massachusetts and Pennsylvania make it harder to complete a hostile merger.

19. Director's Duties, Shareholder Rights laws, Classified Board Laws, Supermajority Laws and Fair Price Laws may affect the merger results.

20. Multiple bidders increase the price of the target. Losing bidders may lose from the reputation of a failed bid.

21. Cash mergers have higher returns; investors must pay taxes on a cash merger. Stock swaps have more risk and a lower probability of completion.

22. International mergers have higher premiums, closer to 12% on announcement.

23. Mergers in the US are typically more common; however, state laws may influence the result.

24. A strategic bidder will pay more for a target than a conglomerate.

25. Hostile mergers have higher returns, on average, around 25-30% on the announcement of the merger for the target firm.

26. D

27. D

28. Buy the target and short the bidder. This trade is only implemented after the merger is announced; otherwise it would be a very speculative strategy.

29. B

30. B

31. C

CH 7 ANSWERS (CONTINUED)

32. Merger arbitrage is very specific and defined. Convertible arbitrage has many facets and types of risk. Convertible arbitrage has far more leverage, but similar market risk.

33. B

34. B

35. C

36. B

37. A

38. A

CHAPTER 8
CONVERTIBLE BOND ARBITRAGE
HEDGE FUNDS

QUESTIONS

1. What is the basic strategy for the convertible bond arbitrage?

2. What are the average returns to the convertible bond strategy?

3. What is the average volatility of the convertible bond hedge funds?

4. How do the levels of skewness compare with long short or short only strategies?

5. What is the average skewness and average kurtosis of the convertible bond strategy?

6. How does the skewness of convertible bond arbitrage compare with the skewness of merger arbitrage?

7. On a graph of credit risk and market risk where would the convertible bond hedge funds be located?

8. What was the drawdown for the convertible bond arbitrage strategy and how long did it last?

9. What was the worst month for the convertible bond strategy?

10. What types of events affect the returns to convertible arbitrage?

11. What types of strategies may be used to profit in convertible bonds? List six strategies.

12. What percentage of profitable months did the convertible bond arbitrage strategy have over the time periods studied in the textbook?

13. List the types of risk in the convertible bond arbitrage strategy. Which markets will be traded?

14. What types of inefficiencies are exploited in the convertible arbitrage strategy?

CH 8 QUESTIONS (CONTINUED)

15. What methods can be used to price a convertible bond?

16. Which hedging strategies may be useful for the convertible bond hedge fund manager?

17. On a graph of credit risk and market risk where would convertible bond strategies be located relative to merger arbitrage strategies?

18. How is a mortgage-backed security different than a treasury?

19. How is a collateralized debt obligation different than a corporate bond?

20. What is a barbell strategy and how does it compare to a ladder?

21. How is trading credit different than predicting yield curve changes? What types of information are used in each type of trading?

22. How is volatility trading different than credit trading?

23. How is restructuring trading different than yield curve changes?

24. What is the carry trade?

25. Explain the basic strategy that a convertible arbitrage fund uses.

26. The definition of arbitrage is?

27. Create a marketing pitch for a convertible arbitrage fund.

28. A major problem convertible arbitrage funds faced in 2008 was?

29. To execute a convertible arbitrage strategy correctly you must understand
    A. Sharpe Ratios.
    B. The Fama-French model.
    C. Greeks.
    D. IRRs of the new projects.

30. Because bonds have predictable cash flows the strategy has lower risk than equities.
    A.   True
    B.   False

CH 8 QUESTIONS (CONTINUED)

31. Annual volatility rates are higher than the S&P 500.
    A. True
    B. False

32. Convertible arbitrage strategies have betas of
    A. 25%
    B. 75%
    C. 10%
    D. 50%

33. Explain the types of risk.

34. A successful convertible arbitrage strategy is
    A. Nonlinear
    B. Asymmetric
    C. Profiting with hedging
    D. All of the above

35. High Gamma means
    A. Delta will change rapidly.
    B. You must hedge for small changes.
    C. You have lower implied volatilities.
    D. All of the above

36. Convertible Arbitrage funds must hold
    A. Companies with low deltas.
    B. Cash.
    C. Companies with high Vega's.
    D. None of the above

37. The change in convertible prices with respect to the recovery rate is
    A. Omicron
    B. Chi
    C. Vega
    D. Upsilon

38. Small changes in the price are hedged with
    A. Gamma
    B. Rho
    C. Delta
    D. Vega

CH 8 QUESTIONS (CONTINUED)

39. One problem many Convertible Arbitrage managers face is
    A. Analyzing Credit Risk.
    B. Covering shorts.
    C. Calculating Greeks.
    D. Buying and shorting equally.

40. Change in price with respect to volatility is
    A. Vega
    B. Delta
    C. Omicron
    D. None of the above

41. The Black-Scholes model for an American Option uses which variables
    A. The stock price, the risk free rate, the present value of the exercise price, the time.
    B. The stock price, the risk free rate, the dividend, the net present value of the exercise
    C. price, the implied volatility.
    D. The stock price, the time, the risk free rate, the dividend, the net present value of the
    E. exercise price, the implied volatility.
    F. D. The stock price, the time, the risk free rate, the net present value of the exercise price,
    G. the implied volatility.

42. The major difference(s) between an American option and a European option is
    A. When you can exercise the option.
    B. The volumes of the contracts.
    C. The price of the options.
    D. A and C

43. The first derivative of the Black-Scholes model is also known as
    A. The Gamma
    B. The Vega
    C. The Delta
    D. The Omega
    E. Rho
    F. None of the above

CH 8 QUESTIONS (CONTINUED)

44. Which of the following are real types of options
    A. American
    B. European
    C. Bermuda
    D. A and B
    E. All of the above

CHAPTER 8
CONVERTIBLE BOND ARBITRAGE
HEDGE FUNDS

ANSWERS

This Table's data (Relative Value Categories) is used for answering empirical questions of Ch. 8 (Convert. Bond Arb.), Ch. 9 (Fixed Income Arb. - Corporate), and Ch. 11 (Volatility Hedge Funds)

Since Inception	Annual Mean Return	Annual Std.Dev.	Annual Skew	Mean Return	Std. Dev.	Skew	Excess Kurtosis	
S&P 500	7.03%	15.24%	-0.24	0.67%	4.40%	-0.83	1.95	Jan 2005 - Dec 2013
10-Yr T-Bond	4.56%	7.87%	0.18	0.40%	2.27%	0.61	2.02	
CRB Index	-0.15%	18.63%	-0.21	0.14%	5.38%	-0.74	2.32	
MSCI Index	3.98%	16.63%	-0.26	0.44%	4.80%	-0.91	2.21	
Fixed Income-Asset Backed	12.20%	3.64%	-0.22	0.97%	1.05%	-0.78	2.26	
Fixed Income-Corporate	4.74%	6.68%	-1.04	0.41%	1.93%	-3.61	21.00	
Fixed Income-Sovereign	3.51%	8.20%	-1.11	0.32%	2.37%	-3.84	23.31	
Multi-Strategy	7.06%	6.20%	-0.27	0.59%	1.79%	-0.94	9.60	
Real Estate	2.53%	7.81%	-0.27	0.23%	2.25%	-0.95	1.49	
Energy Infrastructure	11.90%	10.80%	-0.32	0.99%	3.12%	-1.11	3.00	
Yield Alternative	8.29%	10.02%	-0.42	0.71%	2.89%	-1.46	4.50	
S&P 500	6.03%	15.94%	-0.19	0.60%	4.60%	-0.65	0.97	Jan 1998 - Dec 2013
10-Yr T-Bond	5.54%	7.80%	0.03	0.48%	2.25%	0.11	1.43	
CRB Index	1.26%	15.42%	-0.22	0.21%	4.45%	-0.75	3.48	
MSCI Index	3.65%	16.29%	-0.22	0.41%	4.70%	-0.75	1.37	
Convertible Arbitrage	1.78%	11.41%	-2.06	0.21%	3.29%	-7.12	69.61	
Relative Value Arbitrage	4.15%	7.00%	-0.82	0.36%	2.02%	-2.83	17.26	
S&P 500	7.41%	14.62%	-0.25	0.69%	4.22%	-0.87	2.27	Jan 2004 - Dec 2013
10-Yr T-Bond	4.56%	7.80%	0.13	0.40%	2.25%	0.46	1.98	
CRB Index	0.93%	17.96%	-0.23	0.22%	5.19%	-0.78	2.58	
MSCI Index	4.83%	15.98%	-0.28	0.50%	4.61%	-0.96	2.55	
Volatility	4.24%	5.09%	-0.65	0.36%	1.47%	-2.25	8.07	

CH 8 ANSWERS (CONTINUED)

1. Buy the convertible bond and short the common stock of the same company.

2. 1.78%

3. 11.41%

4. The arbitrage strategies have higher skewness and kurtosis.

5. -2.06 and 69.61, respectively.

6. Similar

7. On the market risk scale at one (fixed income), on the credit scale 3 usually.

8. -60.39% and 74 months

9. October 2008

10. Liquidity events and flight to quality events.

11. Income arb, volatility arb, skewness arb, credit arb, gamma trading, delta trading, restructuring arb.

12. 67.71%

13. Stock, bond and option markets. Risks include interest rate risk, beta risk, yield curve changes, stock market large losses, volatility changes in options markets, liquidity, credit risk and others.

14. Options in bond contracts are usually mispriced and are the basis for this trade. This is an illiquid market and bond traders do not hold these assets that are long volatility (the option in the bond has value, but most bondholders do not want this volatility).

15. Bond plus call option approach or stock plus put option method.

16. Delta and gamma hedging are useful.

17. Similar in market risk but above merger arbitrage on the credit risk scale.

CH 8 ANSWERS (CONTINUED)

18. MBS provide monthly dividends and are positively correlated to unemployment. MBS usually have 12-13 year duration values.

19. CDO is based on other cash flows not the cash flow from one entire company.

20. A ladder is a strategy of buying many maturities on the yield curve in equal amounts. For instance, an investor would put 10% of the portfolio in 1 year, 2 year, 3 year bonds, etc. A barbell strategy would place 50% in a 10 year bond and 50% in a 1 year bond.

21. Credit changes require specific company analysis, and yield curve changes require macroeconomic forecasting.

22. Volatility trading requires market or liquidity knowledge, and credit requires specific company knowledge on debt.

23. Restructuring is debt and credit related. Yield curve changes are macroeconomic investment related ideas.

24. Borrow from a low interest rate economy and invest in a high interest rate economy (or asset).

25. Buy the convertible bond and short the common stock.

26. A profitable trade that requires no capital or risk.

27. It is a low volatility strategy with higher returns than a bond index.

28. The shorting ban.

29. C

30. True

31. False

32. C

33. Stock, Bond, and Options markets.

CH 8 ANSWERS (CONTINUED)

34. A

35. A

36. D

37. A

38. C

39. D

40. A

41. C

42. D

43. C

44. E

CHAPTER 9
FIXED INCOME ARBITRAGE, MORTGAGE BACKED SECURITIES AND COLLATERALIZED DEBT OBLIGATIONS

QUESTIONS

1. What is the difference between a mortgage-backed security and a treasury bond?

2. What is the difference between a corporate bond and a federal government bond?

3. What is the difference between a municipal bond and a federal treasury bond?

4. What is a barbell strategy?

5. What is a ladder?

6. Graph the yield curve for treasury bonds. Above that graph, graph the yield curve for debt that is rated AAA.

7. What is the fisher equation?

8. If inflation increases what happens to the nominal interest rates?

9. When interest rates increase what happens to the price of the bonds?

10. Which have more interest rate risk, long-term bonds or short-term bonds?

11. Which have more reinvestment rate risk, long-term bonds or short-term bonds?

12. What are TIPs?

13. Is a bond mutual fund less risky than buying individual bonds?

14. What is the average return on fixed income arbitrage, corporate?

15. What is the average volatility on fixed income arbitrage strategies, corporate?

CH 9 QUESTIONS (CONTINUED)

16. What is the skewness and kurtosis on fixed income strategies, corporate?

17. What was the largest drawdown and how long did it last for corporate?

18. What was the percentage of profitable trading days for the fixed income arbitrage hedge funds, corporate?

19. How do fixed income arbitrage strategies compare and contrast with convertible arbitrage strategies and merger arbitrage strategies?

20. How do these strategies compare with long short equity and market neutral strategies?

21. Describe mortgage-backed securities.

22. List five ways that mortgage-backed securities are different than other types of fixed income securities.

23. What role does the US government play in the prices of fixed income securities and mortgage backed securities?

24. If the Federal Reserve buys mortgage backed securities, what impact does this have on the prices of these assets? What impact does this have on volatility?

25. If the Federal Reserve discontinues the purchase of mortgage-backed securities, what impact would this have on the market?

26. What is a stripped bond?

27. What is the difference between a 30 year treasury bond and a 29 year treasury bond?

28. What type of option pricing model would a fixed income investor typically use? Why?

29. A fixed income arbitrage fund might short a stock and long a treasury bond.
    a. True
    b. False

CH 9 QUESTIONS (CONTINUED)

30. Compare a distressed lending fund to a fixed income arbitrage fund.

31. Fixed Income Arbitrage funds may long parts of a security while shorting the bond.
    a. True
    b. False

32. Fixed Income funds almost always have perfect arbitrage
    a. True
    b. False

CHAPTER 9
FIXED INCOME ARBITRAGE, MORTGAGE BACKED SECURITIES AND COLLATERALIZED DEBT OBLIGATIONS

ANSWERS

1. A mortgage backed security pays interest monthly while a treasury pays interest semi-annually. A treasury is backed by the Fed and is considered a risk free asset.

2. Corporate bonds have default risk.

3. Municipal bonds are backed by state or local government and the interest is exempt from federal taxes. The interest from a federal bond is exempt from state taxes.

4. Purchasing 50% of the portfolio at endpoint of the yield curve chosen by the investor.

5. Equal distribution across a yield curve. An example would be purchasing 10% of a portfolio at ten successive years.

6. See notes

7. R=r + inflation

8. Nominal rates Increase

9. Decreases

10. Long-term

11. Short-term

12. Treasury inflation protected securities; these securities go up and down with the rate of inflation.

13. Not always because bond mutual fund managers have to reinvest which raises reinvestment rate risk. However, most other types of risk are usually lower in a bond mutual fund.

CH 9 ANSWERS (CONTINUED)

14. 4.74%

15. 6.68%

16. -1.04 and 21.00, respectively

17. -25.8% and 40 months

18. 75.93%

19. All three have a larger skewness than most other types of hedge funds

20. These strategies have more leverage

21. A mortgage backed security pays interest monthly and is positively correlated to the unemployment rate.

22. More cash flows.

     Duration is longer than ten.

     Government frequently intervenes in this market.

     Unemployment rate is correlated.

     Prepayment risk.

23. Government plays a role because the Federal Reserve may buy or sell these securities. Ginnie Mae and Fannie Mae at times have owned 80-90% of all mortgages issued in the United States.

24. Prices and volatility increases when the Federal Reserve changes buying or selling.

25. Interest rates should increase

26. A stripped bond has just the interest payment.

27. There is a large difference in liquidity

28. Binomial model because it's more flexible with cash payments and the up and down movements do not have to be symmetrical.

CH 9 ANSWERS (CONTINUED)

29. False

30. Distressed funds deal with credit and legal risk; it is one type of a fixed income investment. However, you are not able to go short in many distressed lending funds.

31. True

32. False

CHAPTER 10
EVENT DRIVEN AND SPECIAL SITUATION HEDGE FUNDS

QUESTIONS

1. What are the average returns to events such as mergers, layoffs, spinoffs, strikes, restructuring, issue of debt, and issue of new stock and hostile takeovers?

2. How large must abnormal returns be to trade profitably in the financial markets? How is this related to leverage?

3. What are the risk factors for an event on a specific type of company? Are these macroeconomic or firm specific factors?

4. What was the average return for event driven hedge funds since inception?

5. What was the average volatility for event driven hedge funds since inception?

6. What was the skewness and kurtosis for event driven funds since inception?

7. How does the skewness of an event driven fund compare with merger arbitrage and convertible bond arbitrage?

8. On a graph of credit and market risk where would event driven hedge funds be located?

9. How does the event driven strategy compare with market neutral strategies?

10. How do event driven strategies compare with global macro and long short equity?

11. What levels of leverage do event driven hedge funds typically use?

12. When do event driven hedge funds underperform? Which types of economic environments would more likely cause an event driven fund to underperform?

13. What was the drawdown for an event driven fund and how long did it last?

14. If the amount of capital in a strategy doubles in three years, what would happen to the half-life of this strategy?

CH 10 QUESTIONS (CONTINUED)

15. What is the difference between arbitrage and quasi-arbitrage?

16. When does the SEC require disclosure of your intentions in a stock
    A. 15% of the company
    B. 20% of the company
    C. 5% of the company
    D. 10% of the company

17. What can event funds trade Stocks Futures Options All of the above

18. The SEC allows event driven funds to use options, futures and any type of derivative.
    A. True
    B. False

19. Sharpe Ratios for event driven funds are greater than macro funds.
    A. True
    B. False

20. Explain an event that has taken place and how you could profit.

21. The Sharpe Ratios for event driven funds are lower than macro funds.
    A. True
    B. False

CHAPTER 10
EVENT DRIVEN AND SPECIAL SITUATION HEDGE FUNDS

ANSWERS

1. See results.

2. A higher level of profit means that you can use a lower level of leverage. When leverage is not available lower profit strategies go out of business.

3. Firm specific, mergers, restructuring, and take over.

4. 5.49%

5. 6.65%

6. -.43 and 4.92, respectively.

7. It will have similar skewness and kurtosis.

8. Next to merger arbitrage (2, 1) and (1, 1).

9. Event driven strategies have more market risk, more skew, and more leverage.

10. Event driven funds typically have less market risk and more event risk.

11. One to two X.

12. Event driven funds underperform when there are fewer corporate events and liquidity events such as a flight to quality.

13. -25.8% and 77 months.

14. The profit would decrease in this industry.

CH 10 ANSWERS (CONTINUED)

15. Arbitrage has no risk while Quasi has small amounts of risk and you use leverage to enhance returns.

16. C

17. D

18. True

19. True

20. Buy the common stock of corporations that successfully restructure or buy the target stock in a merger.

21. False

CHAPTER 11
QUANTITATIVE TRADING AND VOLATILITY HEDGE FUNDS

QUESTIONS

1. What types of risk are being hedged?

2. What is tail risk?

3. What is a volatility spread?

4. Why have volatility funds increased in popularity in the last decade?

5. When most assets decrease in value which types of securities will increase in value?

6. If a trader buys an option is the position long or short volatility?

7. What is the VIX?

8. Why is the VIX a difficult security to trade to protect the value of your portfolio?

9. What methods or tools might a volatility trader use?

10. What is the difference between trading in the futures markets and the options market when concerned about volatility?

11. What is a cross hedge?

12. What was the average return for volatility hedge funds?

13. What was the average volatility for volatility funds?

14. What was the average skewness and kurtosis for volatility hedge funds?

15. How do volatility funds compare with global macro funds?

16. How do volatility funds compare with managed futures?

CH 11 QUESTIONS (CONTINUED)

17. How does the skewness of volatility funds compare with the skewness of convertible arbitrage and merger arbitrage funds?
18. What was the largest drawdown for volatility funds and how long did it last?

    What was the percentage of profitable days trading for volatility funds? How does this compare with merger arbitrage and long short equity funds?
19. What types of events could cause large changes in the value of a volatility fund?

20. What is Gamma trading?

21. What is Vega trading?

22. What types of economic environments would volatility funds outperform other assets?

23. Do volatility funds destabilize financial markets?

24. Are volatility strategies mean convergence strategies, typically? If not, are they sustainable?

25. Prior to the introduction of volatility hedge funds which strategies in the options and futures markets could an investor use to hedge volatility?

26. Volatility that tracks the S&P is known as the
    a. VIA
    b. VAI
    c. VVV
    d. VIX

27. The volatility of the S&P has weekly percent changes similar to stock.
    a. True
    b. False

28. Explain why a volatility fund would be a good place for institutional investors. Also, tell why institutions stay away from volatility funds that have less than 150 AUM.

CH 11 QUESTIONS (CONTINUED)

29. Volatility traders often make money
    a. Delta hedging
    b. Vega hedging
    c. Gamma hedging
    d. All of the above

30. Compare a volatility fund to a managed futures fund.

31. Lock-up periods for high frequency trading funds are relatively short.
    a. True
    b. False

32. The term "quote slamming" means
    a. Bidding up a price and then canceling the order.
    b. Not knowing the volumes in dark pools.
    c. Shorting after hours trading.
    d. Using an algorithm to increase volumes of a stock when they go below a certain volume.

33. Explain the major differences between a high frequency trading fund and a "quant" fund.

34. High frequency trading funds often account for a significant level of volume on exchanges.
    a. True
    b. False

CHAPTER 11
QUANTITATIVE TRADING AND VOLATILITY HEDGE FUNDS

ANSWERS

1. Frequently, volatility and tail risk are being hedged in volatility funds. A quant fund may have very specific risk dimensions depending on the approach. If a momentum strategy is used, then risk tends to increase.

2. Tail risk is the risk that extremely large loses occur in the portfolio.

3. A volatility spread is the sale and purchase of volatility. It is a method of going long volatility and short volatility to limit the exposure of volatility in the portfolio. Similar to a bull or bear spread an investor can go long or short volatility. The spread just caps the gain or loss from a change in volatility.

4. When there is a crisis, all assets seem to decrease in value, except volatility. Therefore, investors are using volatility as an asset class. It is useful for hedging.

5. Volatility increases, as well as, put options, shorting, etc.

6. Long

7. Volatility index on the S&P 500.

8. The roll over each month implies a higher price. The cost is increasing and the construct of the contract uses a weighted average of all options in the S&P 500 (roughly). The use of all of these option classes may not be optimal as a hedging unit.

9. Straddles, strips, straps, strangles, volatility spreads, butterfly spreads, condors, etc.

10. Futures positions mark to market every day and the margin calls can put the trader out of a position. The buyer of an option just has to continue holding the security.

11. Using one asset, X to hedge another asset Y.

CH 11 ANSWERS (CONTINUED)

12. 4.24%

13. 5.09%

14. -.65 and 8.47, respectively.

15. Both seem to outperform other assets during a crisis. Both are usually long volatility.

16. Managed futures and volatility funds may be long volatility and outperform during a crisis.

17. Lower skewness for volatility funds.

18. -15.37% and 55 months. 73.33% profitable days.

19. Liquidity events, banking crisis, inflation in a major currency, default risk.

20. Trading to hedge large changes in the underlying stock price so that the portfolio does not lose much in value.

21. A hedge to prevent losses in a portfolio due to small changes in the portfolio.

22. During a crisis or the threat of a crisis a volatility fund will usually outperform other funds.

23. Volatility funds provide capital for trading volatility. This means that they would normally provide stability for the system.

24. Most hedge funds are using mean convergent strategies, since they are more common trades that are profitable. Long shots and extreme trades need more capital to sustain themselves in the marketplace; otherwise the hedge fund will go out of business.

25. Straddles, butterfly spreads, condors, strangles, etc.

26. D

27. A

CH 11 ANSWERS (CONTINUED)

28. Tail risk can be hedged and institutional investors are willing to pay for this protection. If the asset size is too small, then the protection may be too expensive.

29. D (especially C).

30. Volatility funds are long volatility usually and so are managed futures. Managed futures have liquid transparent assets; volatility traders have more complex underlying securities.

31. A

32. A

33. A high frequency trading fund will execute trades within seconds; a quant fund will use statistical techniques but will usually have a longer time horizon and make far fewer trades.

34. A (sometimes 30%- 50%).

CHAPTER 12
THE BINOMIAL MODEL

QUESTIONS

1. What is the hedge ratio if the stock price is $100, the exercise price is $110, U equals 1.3 and D equals .9?

2. If the risk free interest rate is 5% and T is 6 months, what is the value of the call option in time one for the option in the problem above?

3. What does U represent in the binomial model?

4. What does P represent in the binomial model?

5. Suppose that D equals .8, U equals 1.2, the risk free rate is 4%, the time to expiration is 3 months, the stock price is $40 and the strike price is $44, what is the price of the call option? What would be the value of a put option?

6. If the investor uses a value for U and D that is too small what impact will that have on the hedge ratio? If the values are too large what impact would that have on the hedge ratio?

7. Does the binomial model assume stock returns are symmetric?

8. What variables are in the binomial option pricing model?

9. What variables are in the Black-Scholes model?

10. Calculate the probability, P, in the binomial model if the risk-free rate is 3%, the time to expiration is 4 months, U equals 1.1 and D equals .8. If U changes to 1.3 how does this change the value of P?

11. What assumptions are used for Delta hedging?

12. If the hedge ratio is .5 what is the underlying stock and call option position?

13. What is the payoff graph for a covered call with a naked call?

14. Why are risk preferences not used in the binomial model?

CHAPTER 12
THE BINOMIAL MODEL

ANSWERS

1. H = (20-0)/(130-90) = .5

2. P = (1.025-.9) / (1.3-.9) = .31 and 1-P = .69, therefore, Vc = [.31(20) + .69(0)]e-rT = $6.27 (.975) = $6.12 .

3. The upside volatility.

4. The probability of success or stock price above the exercise price. It is actually not the actual probability, but a risk neutral probability.

5. $40

6. The hedge ratio will result in not having enough insurance. The investor is under hedged.

7. No, U and D do not have to be symmetric. This is a difference between the Black-Scholes model and the binomial model.

8. The same factors used in the Black-Scholes model; however, volatility in the binomial model is captured using U and D. The factors include the stock price, strike price, time, risk free rate, volatility and dividends.

9. The same variables as in problem 8.

10. P = [e(.03)(.333) - .8]/(1.1-.8) = 4/.3 = (1.01-.8)/.3 = .21/.3 = .7, if U increases then the denominator increases.   P = .21/(1.3-.8) = .21/.5 = .42. The value of a call option increases, but the probability decreases.

11. Assume the market will allow continuous trading to constantly hedge. If the market fails or there is not enough volume, then the trades cannot be executed.

12. Buy 500 shares of stock and write call options on 1000 shares of stock.

CH 12 ANSWERS (CONTINUED)

13. See graphs, but the final position is a covered call and a naked call. This combination is similar to writing a straddle. It is risk free around the current stock price, however, it has a great deal of risk and the position cannot be traded.

14. The ability to set up risk free positions allows pricing without investor preferences. The rate of return on a risk free asset is known. Arbitrage prevents the prices from being too large or small.

CHAPTER 13
PRIVATE EQUITY, VENTURE CAPITAL, PIPES, AND DISTRESSED LENDING

QUESTIONS

1. What is the J Curve?

2. What is the primary type of company a VC fund attempts to purchase?

3. How is the type of firm a PE firm wants, different from what a VC firm wants?

4. What is the diversification model of a VC firm?

5. What levels of corporate finance are needed in PE and VC firms versus merger arbitrage or convertible arbitrage funds?

6. What does PIPE mean?

7. How is PIPE investing different than distressed lending?

8. What types of expertise are needed in distressed lending?

9. How are PE, VC, PIPEs and distressed lending different than merger arbitrage or market neutral or long short strategies?

10. A private equity fund generates the most cash flows
    a. Early in the J curve.
    b. In the middle of the J curve.
    c. Later in the J curve.Where the J curve starts to shift upward.

11. Lock-ups are usually
    a. 1-3 years
    b. 3-4 years
    c. 4-5 years
    d. 5-7 years

CH 13 QUESTIONS (CONTINUED)

12. Private Equity returns have been
    a. Less than global macro.
    b. Greater than Market Neutral.
    c. Less than Event.
    d. None of the above

13. Private Equity lost money do to undisciplined investors in 2008.
    a. True
    b. False

14. In recent years Venture Capitalists have had problems with
    a. Finding enough good deals in American companies.
    b. Working with investment banks to go public.
    c. Raising Capital.
    d. Using up their "dry powder."

15. Lock-up periods for Private Equity and Market Neutral are
    a. Longer for Private Equity.
    b. Shorter for Private Equity.
    c. Approximately the same for both strategies.
    d. None of the above

16. The major difference between Venture Capital and Private Equity is
    a. Liquidity
    b. Volatility
    c. Leverage
    d. Company start ups

17. Explain the process that a venture capital fund would go through to buy a company.

18. A common technique(s) used by venture capital funds against Angel investors is
    a. Quote slamming
    b. Dark pool trading
    c. Cramdown
    d. All of the above

19. What are the major advantages to running a Venture Capital fund?

CHAPTER 13
PRIVATE EQUITY, VENTURE CAPITAL, PIPES, AND DISTRESSED LENDING

ANSWERS

1. A relationship seen in Private Equity funds that indicate initial returns are negative as the firm is investing in a company. The returns take time because there is a long process to improve the company.

2. Startup companies and many are technology companies.

3. A PE firm is looking for a company with positive cash flows and already has an established product. The PE firm wants to improve the company and its cash flows, not create a new product or company (necessarily). A VC is looking for startup companies with great potential to enter a market or industry.

4. A VC firm may invest in 30 different startups and hope that 5 firms profit, with a very large payoff if each one succeeds. A PE firm may invest in only 3 companies over a 10 year period.

5. Both strategies require a great deal of corporate finance knowledge (versus investments knowledge for many hedge funds).

6. Private Investment in a Public Equity.

7. PIPES invest in equity and PIPES have more liquid underlying assets. A PIPE investment may be in a less liquid preferred stock of a liquid common stock. Distressed lending will involve debt from a less liquid company. Laws or courts may prevent the distressed lender from selling earlier (perhaps wait for 2 or 3 years to sell the investment). A PIPE may have a contractual agreement not to sell for a limited time period.

8. Credit expertise and legal knowledge.

9. PE, VC, PIPE and distressed lending are all long term investments that are primarily long positions (with very few, if any, short positions).

10. C

CH 13 ANSWERS (CONTINUED)

11. B

12. A

13. A

14. B

15. A

16. D

17. The process would start with an entrepreneur, then possibly an Angel investor, then the VC would enter the process, then another bidder or an IPO may take place.

18. C

19. The opportunity to profit while investing and effecting change in companies that will change or define an industry.

CHAPTER 14
GLOBAL MACRO FUNDS

QUESTIONS

1. When are Global Macro Funds more popular with investors?

2. How are Global Macro Funds different than other hedge funds?

3. Should a Global Macro Fund tell investors when they are investing more capital into different markets?

4. What levels of leverage do Global Macro Funds typically use? What is their implied leverage?

5. What types of strategies do Global Macro Funds imitate if you were to describe it in option pricing terms?

6. How do investors keep Global Macro Hedge Fund managers accountable?

7. How is due diligence different for a Global Macro Fund than a Merger Arbitrage Fund?

8. How are Long Short Funds different than Global Macro Funds?

9. How is a general idea different than a specific idea in terms of investing? Describe differences between Top Down analysis and Bottom Up analysis.

10. List advantages Global Macro Funds have over other types of funds and describe these advantages on an efficient frontier.

11. What disadvantages do Global Macro Funds have relative to other funds?

CHAPTER 14
GLOBAL MACRO FUNDS

ANSWERS

1. After a crisis Global Macro Funds are more popular because large changes in volatility continue and returns across sectors may vary widely. The Global Macro manager can exploit those differences for higher returns.

2. Global Macro Funds have a more inclusive mandate allowing the hedge fund manager much more discretion across assets and countries.

3. No, some of those investors will mimic the strategy and release the information to other investors. Other investors will use that information to make similar investments and decrease the returns. In addition, some investors will use the information to make it more difficult for the manager to exit the position and, therefore, lose money on the trade.

4. A level of 1X to 3X is common. Implied leverage will vary because the choice of asset market will have an impact on the level of leverage used. For instance, an investment in commodities will typically have more implied leverage because of the leverage allowed by regulators.

5. Global Macro performs better during a crisis, therefore, many investors view the strategy as long volatility, similar to a straddle.

6. They vote with their money and do not allocate capital to underperformers. In addition, they may withdraw funds previously invested.

7. Due diligence for a merger arbitrage fund is more specific to one strategy and the underlying firm. Global Macro funds have issues relating to the implementation of many strategies. It is difficult to be an expert in many areas.

8. Long Short funds typically stay in one asset class and Global Macro funds usually go across asset classes such as: stocks, bonds, commodities, and currencies.

CH 14 ANSWERS (CONTINUED)

9. A Global Macro manager may correctly infer that an asset class will increase or decrease in value, however, to implement the strategy may take more expertise. The correct asset may not exist and may have to be created by another willing market participant. Top Down analysis looks at the global macroeconomic picture and attempts to anticipate changes in security returns. Bottom Up analysis looks at the specific stock or asset and attempts to determine whether this specific asset is underpriced. Top Down analysis may involve more economic analysis and timing aspects and Bottom Up is more security selection.

10. The ability to move across asset classes is a huge advantage for Global Macro Fund managers. On an efficient frontier, the Global Macro strategy will have the ability to change correlations and the advantage of investing in more market opportunities. Having more options to invest expands the efficient frontier.

11. The hedge fund manager cannot communicate the asset class or specific investment to investors and this makes it more difficult, if not impossible, for the investor to determine THE optimal allocation.

CHAPTER 15
CURRENCY HEDGE FUNDS

QUESTIONS

1. The three daily factors that affect all currencies do not include
   _____?
   a. Interest rates
   b. Inflation
   c. GDP
   d. Oil

2. A commodity currency has _____ volatility than a hard currency.
   a. Lower
   b. Higher
   c. The same
   d. None of the above

3. The business model of a currency affects the actions of
   _____ .
   a. Central bankers of the economy
   b. Hedge fund managers
   c. Central bankers of other countries
   d. All the above

4. The hard currencies of the world do not include which of the following?
   a. Swiss franc
   b. Chinese RMB or Yuan
   c. Mexican peso
   d. Russian ruble
   e. All the above

CH 15 QUESTIONS (CONTINUED)

5. The reserve currency of the world is:
   a. Euro
   b. Yen
   c. Pound
   d. US Dollar
   e. Chinese Yuan

6. List the important factors that affect the currency values and discuss how each variable impacts the value of a currency.

7. What is the carry trade? What strategies might lower risk in a carry trade?

8. The carry trade is a trade where the source of capital is in the _____ interest rate economy, and the investment is in the _____ interest rate economy.
   a. Low, High
   b. High, Low
   c. Rising, Falling
   d. Falling, Rising
   e. None of the above

9. Does the evolution of value added trade put pressure on central banks to increase or decrease exchange rates or the value of a currency?

10. What are the types of businesses that benefit from an increase in the value of the Euro relative to the US Dollar? Which participants in the economy benefit when the value of the Euro falls relative to the US Dollar?

CH 15 QUESTIONS (CONTINUED)

11. Which of the following participants benefit from an increase in the value of the Euro versus the US Dollar?
    a. German automakers
    b. Spanish wine producers
    c. US automakers
    d. US importers
    e. None of the above

12. Which of the following would be the first to make public statements on exchange rates and the US Dollar being too high relative to the Japanese Yen?
    a. Toyota
    b. Mercedes
    c. General Motors
    d. Honda
    e. Fiat

CHAPTER 15
CURRENCY HEDGE FUNDS

ANSWERS

1. D

2. B

3. D

4. E

5. D

6. Interest rates, inflation and economic activity (GDP) all affect the daily values of currencies. As interest rates in an economy rise, money from other countries is attracted to the higher yield and enters the country. This causes an increase in value in the currency. As inflation rises, the purchasing power decreases and the value of the currency decreases relative to other currencies. As economic activity rises, more currency is needed for transactions, therefore the demand and value for the currency rises.

7. The carry trade is a trade in which you borrow money from a low interest rate economy and invest it in a high interest rate economy. Borrowing money from an economy with low interest rates and in an economy that attempts to keep its currency value low to sell exports may lower the risk of the carry trade. The central bank has an incentive to keep the exchange rate low and this lowers the risk for the carry trade.

8. A

CH 15 ANSWERS (CONTINUED)

9. As an economy progresses to higher value added goods, the central bank may change the currency policy to try to appreciate or increase the value of a currency. This allows importers to buy cheaper goods and then add value and then export to other countries. The imports are cheaper if the central bank increases the value of the domestic currency.

10. US automakers can sell more cars if the value of the Euro rises relative to the US Dollar. Foreign imports are cheaper for Europeans when the value of the Euro rises. European automakers find it easier to sell cars in the US when the Euro falls relative to the US Dollar.

11. C

12. C

CHAPTER 16
COMMODITY HEDGE FUNDS AND MANAGED FUTURES

QUESTIONS

1. It is common for a managed futures fund to have a 3 year lock up?
   a. True
   b. False

2. Commodity hedge funds and managed futures funds both trade commodities and both have the same regulators?
   a. True
   b. False

3. Commodity hedge funds are typically _____ volatility.
   a. Short
   b. Long
   c. Both

4. Commodity hedge funds have a lot of skew?
   a. True
   b. False

5. Commodity hedge funds perform _____ relative to most hedge funds, during a crisis.
   a. Better
   b. Worse
   c. The same
   d. None of the above

6. Agricultural commodity hedge funds have _____ skew than metal hedge funds.
   a. Higher
   b. Lower
   c. The same
   d. None of the above

CH 16 QUESTIONS (CONTINUED)

7. Which of the following would be the best protection against inflation risk?
    a. Wheat
    b. Oil
    c. Gold
    d. Milk
    e. Feeder cattle

8. Which of the following assets is the most correlated with the S&P 500?
    a. Orange juice
    b. Gold
    c. Copper
    d. Aluminum

9. The time periods when commodity hedge funds do not perform very well usually have _____.
    a. High interest rates
    b. High exchange rates
    c. High volatility
    d. High stock returns
    e. High long term bond returns

10. Tail risk is _____ .
    a. The risk of a large gain and a large loss
    b. The risk of a large loss
    c. The risk of an increase in volatility
    d. The risk of a commodity trade not being completed
    e. Liquidity risk

CH 16 QUESTIONS (CONTINUED)

11. When a central bank increases the money supply or uses a quantitative easing program such as buying assets in the financial markets, this causes _____ to decrease.
    a. Stock prices
    b. Bond prices
    c. Volatility
    d. Liquidity
    e. None of the above

12. A traditional portfolio manager might prefer to add a _____ commodity hedge fund prior to a _____ commodity hedge fund, due to correlations.
    a. Trend following, discretionary
    b. Discretionary, trend following
    c. Metals, agricultural
    d. Might not have any preference

CHAPTER 16
COMMODITY HEDGE FUNDS AND
MANAGED FUTURES

ESSAY QUESTIONS

1. Do managed futures allow the investor to diversify?

2. What is the average volatility of a managed futures fund?

3. What types of assets are traded in a managed futures fund?

4. What regulators affect managed futures fund?

5. Why do managed funds increase in popularity after a financial crisis?

6. During a large market decrease how do most managed funds perform? How do most funds perform during good times?

7. What is the average return to the managed futures hedge fund and a commodity hedge fund?

8. What is the average volatility for a commodity hedge fund and managed futures funds?

9. What is the average skew and kurtosis for a CTA or managed futures fund?

10. How do commodity hedge funds and managed futures compare with long short equity?

11. How do commodity hedge funds and managed futures compare with convertible arbitrage and merger arbitrage strategies?

12. What is the largest drawdown for CTAs or managed futures funds?

13. How long did the drawdown last for CTAs?

CH 16 ESSAY QUESTIONS (CONTINUED)

14. When do managed futures tend to underperform?

15. List two types of managed futures strategies. How are quantitative strategies different than others?

16. How do Black box strategies compare with discretionary strategies?
17. How transparent are the assets for a managed futures fund?

18. Is pricing difficult, compared with other types of alternative assets, for a managed futures fund?

19. Which assets and which markets would a managed futures funds trade?

20. Are commodity funds long or short volatility?

21. What factor does momentum play in managed futures funds?

22. What factor do interest rates play in commodity hedge funds and managed futures returns?

CHAPTER 16
COMMODITY HEDGE FUNDS AND MANAGED FUTURES

ESSAY ANSWERS

1. Investors can diversify quickly with managed futures.

2. Managed futures funds usually are long volatility and benefit when volatility rises.

3. Stock indices, currencies, agricultural commodities, metals, bonds, interest rates, commodities

4. CFTC, NFA

5. Managed futures tend to have positive returns during a crisis and investors seek positive returns so they invest in managed futures during these time periods.

6. They outperform stock markets and tend to have large positive returns because they are long volatility. During good times they tend to underperform the stock market.

7. CTAs managed futures have a 5.44% average return and commodity funds have an average return of 4.97%.

8. The CTA volatility was 8.48% and the volatility for commodity hedge funds was 7.39%.

9. The average skew for CTAs was .11skew and for commodity funds it was .24 skew (positive skew)

10. Managed futures and commodity funds tend to do well during a crisis, when the long short equity is losing money. They underperform when long short equity is doing well and stock indices are doing well.

CH 16 ESSAY ANSWERS (CONTINUED)

11. The skew for managed futures and commodity hedge funds are positive. The skew for convert arbitrage and merger arbitrage strategies are negative.

12. CTA drawdown was -23.96% and for commodity funds it varied from -15% to -56%.

13. 66 months or 5.5 years

14. When volatility is low and when the stock market is doing well.

15. Discretionary and quantitative. Quants follow a specific set of rules.

16. Quant strategies do not try to pick a top or bottom and are based on momentum usually. The pattern of returns is different for quants versus discretionary traders. Discretionary traders hit returns from a top or bottom faster but then they leave earlier. Quants follow momentum and, therefore, get returns later than discretionary traders but tend to trade later with the trend.

17. Very transparent they trade every second on a futures market.

18. Pricing is easy and transparent. The futures exchanges have the prices available all the time.

19. Commodities and any contracts on futures exchanges (bonds, stock indices, currencies).

20. Long usually

21. Large factor for quant funds.

22. Higher interest rates decrease the demand for commodities because commodities don't pay dividends. The opportunity cost of leaving money in commodities is higher when interest rates are higher.

CHAPTER 16
COMMODITY HEDGE FUNDS AND
MANAGED FUTURES

MULTIPLE CHOICE ANSWERS

1. D

2. B

3. C

4. B

5. C

6. D

7. D

8. A

9. D

10. B

11. A

12. B

13. B

14. They would talk about their risk management, trend trading and long volatility exposure.

15. Their returns tend to be higher during a crisis.

16. High frequency funds tend to do more arbitrage related trades and tend to be short volatility, while commodity funds tend to be long volatility and are exposed to longer risks thru time.

17. B

CH 16 MULTIPLE CHOICE ANSWERS (CONTINUED)

18. D

19. B

20. Math or stat oriented people

21. Collectibles are much smaller markets and rely on limited supply and continual popularity in demand for an asset. Commodities can be used as an input in producing or consuming an asset. Commodities are more liquid than collectibles usually. Collectibles may be better at maintaining value during times of inflation.

22. Pecuniary returns are non-monetary returns from owning an asset: bragging rights, status symbol, etc.

23. Commodities are usually benefitting from an increase in volatility and are usually less liquid than most financial instruments.

CHAPTER 17
EMERGING MARKET HEDGE FUNDS

ANSWERS

1. C with higher skew being positive skew

2. D

3. C

4. B

5. B

6. B

7. B

8. B

9. A

CHAPTER 18
SCANDALS AND TRENDS IN THE HEDGE FUND INDUSTRY

QUESTIONS

1. What caused LTCM to fail?

2. Is it easier for con men to operate in good times or bad times?

3. When are global macro funds more popular?

4. What factors allow for the mispricing of hedge fund assets?

5. Who are the primary clients of hedge funds today?

6. Was Bernie Madoff a hedge fund manager?

7. What is due diligence?

8. What are the four steps for creating a hedge fund?

9. Why is actual leverage and listed leverage different?

10. What levels of transparency do investors need?

11. How are individual wealthy clients different than pension funds?

CHAPTER 18
SCANDALS AND TRENDS IN THE
HEDGE FUND INDUSTRY

ANSWERS

1. Too much leverage, markets closed and delta hedging was not possible; mean convergent strategies require the correct means.

2. Easier in good times.

3. After a crisis.

4. Complex securities, illiquid securities, lack of transparency and asymmetric information are some reasons for mispricing.

5. Pension Funds.

6. No

7. Research to make sure the idea and strategy make sense and that the hedge fund manager and her/his team can implement the strategy effectively today and in the future.

8. See section 3, page 200.

9. Actual leverage does not include the leverage in a derivatives contract. The balance sheet will not fully describe every contract the firm is trading.

10. Enough to allocate assets efficiently and enough to prevent fraud.

11. Pension funds allocate funds differently and are usually more sophisticated in terms of quantitative concepts. Risk management techniques of hedge funds tend to be much more complex.

CHAPTER 19
HEDGE FUND BUSINESS PLANS

QUESTIONS

1. What percent of assets are currently in hedge funds on a world basis?

2. What percent of wealthy US clients in single family offices are wealth creators?

3. What percent of wealth creators invest in Private Equity?

4. What percent of wealth creators invest in hedge funds?

5. What are major differences between Private Equity and hedge funds (even though many people categorize them as similar investments)?

6. What percent of wealth preservers invest in Private Equity?

7. What is the tax difference between a master feeder structure and an onshore/offshore structure?

8. What is a gate?

9. What is a hurdle rate?

10. What is a threshold level or high water mark?

11. What is the function of a prime broker?

12. What is the function of an administrator?

13. What legal fees would a hedge fund confront?

14. What is the role of the auditor?

15. What difference does it make if you choose a quality auditor versus an auditor that no one has ever heard of in the industry?

16. What is Regulation S?

17. What is Regulation D?

CH 19 QUESTIONS (CONTINUED)

18. Discuss the concerns institutions have investing in small funds and explain headline risk.

19. Explain what a minimum withdrawal request is and why funds use them.

20. What is a "key person event"?

21. What is disregarded when a "key person event" situation takes place?
    a. Management fees
    b. Lock-up periods
    c. Initial investment
    d. Assets under management fees only

22. If you are doing business with the cheapest prime broker the most important thing to remember in most cases is
    a. It is easier to raise money.
    b. You save money in the long run.
    c. Money leaves faster during a crisis.
    d. It is harder to raise money.

23. Many funds use accountants from within to do their auditing.
    a. True
    b. False

24. Institutions, such as pension funds, prefer to see what percent of your net-worth invested in your hedge fund.
    a. 10%
    b. 50%
    c. 70%
    d. As much as possible

25. Most hedge funds are used for hedging.
    a. True
    b. False

26. Which strategy would you like to implement and why? Explain how you would handle the disadvantages of starting up your fund.

27. Performance fees are starting to decrease.
    a. True
    b. False

CH 19 QUESTIONS (CONTINUED)

28. What do you think will happen to the number of hedge funds in the U.S in the next five years and why?

29. Sharpe Ratios are important when measuring performance of mutual fund and hedge fund managers.
    a. True
    b. False

30. What level of annual income would it take to invest in a hedge fund?
    a. 200,000
    b. 300,000
    c. 100,000
    d. 250,000

31. What is the prime broker's role in starting and maintaining a hedge fund?

32. Prime Brokers focus on research as well.
    a. True
    b. False

33. If hedge funds are known for keeping their strategies proprietary why would they outline their basic strategies in their marketing pitch?

CHAPTER 19
HEDGE FUND BUSINESS PLANS

ANSWERS

1.   2%

2.   70%

3.   50%

4.   90%

5.   PE firms tend to have very long term liquidity concerns. Hedge funds have shorter liquidity provisions, so lock ups tend to be shorter for hedge funds.

6.   50%

7.   Replication of trading costs may occur with 2 separate entities and tax implications may involve trading costs.

8.   A limit placed on investors regarding how much money they can pull out of a hedge fund over a period of time.

9.   The rate the hedge fund manager must outperform to obtain a performance fee (20% usually).

10.   The high water mark is the previous high return level of the fund.

11.   A prime broker has many functions; however, today lending money for shorting is the primary business model.

12.   To handle day to day accounting and business practices.

13.   Set up fees for most funds and some funds require legal expertise (distressed lending and PIPES).

CH 19 ANSWERS (CONTINUED)

14. To ensure safety for investors and the proper valuation of securities in some cases. New and previous investors need the auditor to correctly state the value of the assets. If assets are valued too highly, new investors will overpay when they enter a fund (thus their returns will be lower). If assets are valued too low, then previous investors will obtain lower returns, since new investors will be obtaining new shares for a lower price than the actual value.

15. Establish pension funds will not invest in your fund. The quality of the auditor matters a great deal in terms of safety for the investor.

16. Regulation D is an SEC regulation governing private placement exemptions. It allows (usually) smaller companies to raise capital through the sale of equity or debt securities without having to register those securities with the SEC.

17. Regulation S is an SEC regulation that allows publicly traded companies not to register stocks sold outside the United States to foreign investors. This regulation was passed in 1990 and was intended to encourage foreign investors to purchase American stocks in order to increase the liquidity of American markets.

18. A small hedge fund may have fewer people and the outcome may be less controllable. Headline risk is the probability that the investment ends up as a headline in the news media. Pension funds are subject to political constraints that limit their ability to invest.

19. A minimum may be stated for administrative reasons.

20. A Key Person is someone that would affect the value of the portfolio substantially if they were missing from the firm. A Key Person clause allows the investor (or pension fund) to withdraw funds if the Key Person leaves for any reason.

21. B

22. C

CH 19 QUESTIONS (CONTINUED)

23. B

24. D

25. B

26. Your preferences and strategies listed.

27. A, somewhat.

28. Probably increase, since so few assets are performing well many pension funds need to search for alternative investments.

29. False for Hedge Fund managers.

30. D

31. The prime broker may introduce investors to the hedge fund manager. The trading platform may be provided for lower cost if the hedge fund is a regular client. The prime broker may provide capital for shorting stocks, etc.

32. B

33. Investors need enough transparency to make informed and safe decisions. This keeps fraud out of the industry, as well.

Made in the USA
Las Vegas, NV
17 February 2024

85896711R00063